IMAGINING THE REAL

Imagining the Real

AMOS N. WILDER

WIPF & STOCK · Eugene, Oregon

Wipf and Stock Publishers
199 W 8th Ave, Suite 3
Eugene, OR 97401

Imagining the Real
By Wilder, Amos and Hawkins, Peter S.
Copyright©1978 by Wilder, Amos
ISBN 13: 978-1-62564-394-0
Publication date 1/3/2014
Previously published by Possum Press, 1978

SERIES FOREWORD TO THE AMOS N. WILDER LIBRARY

GIVEN THE SUPERFLUITY OF books in the world, there has to be a compelling reason to reissue those that have gone out of print. Most often a curious reader can rely successfully on interlibrary loan or Google Books to gain access to what the publishing world has otherwise let drop. But this piecemeal retrieval is not sufficient when an author, rather than a single volume, warrants being brought back into circulation; when there is a whole body of work deserving of a fresh audience. Such is the case with Amos Niven Wilder (1895–1993), whose prodigious writing, spanning the better part of a century, claims our attention with its extraordinary variety of genres (poetry, essay, and memoir) and disciplines (biblical study, literary criticism, theology).

First, the man behind the publications. A gift for writing and a passion for literature were very much in the family's DNA. Named for his newspaper-publisher father, Amos was the eldest of five, four of whom distinguished them as writers. Most famous of them was his only brother, the playwright and novelist Thornton Wilder, about whom he wrote "Thornton Wilder and His Public" in 1980. Educated at Yale University, from which he eventually received four degrees, he also undertook biblical and theological studies in France and Belgium but most importantly at Mansfield College, Oxford, where he encountered the likes of Albert Schweitzer (*The Quest of the Historical Jesus*) and C.H. Dodd (renown for the notion of "realized eschatology," wherein the end is not near but now). These years of schooling launched his career as a distinguished New Testament scholar at Andover-Newton Theological Seminary, the Chicago Theological Seminary and the University of Chicago, and finally at Harvard Divinity School. Yet perhaps more crucial to his personal development than this academic training was his service in World War I, during which time he served as a volunteer ambulance driver in France and Macedonia (receiving the *Croix de guerre*) and later saw significant action as a corporal with the U.S. Army field artillery in France. That the "Great War" shaped his life and career is suggested by the works that bracket his publications: his first book, a collection of poems, *Battle Retrospect* (1923), and his very last, *Armageddon Revisited: A World War I Journal* (1994). Both bear witness to a traumatic wartime experience that neither destroyed him nor ever let him go.

For many, the trenches marked the end of faith, but not for Wilder. Upon his discharge he went to Yale Divinity School, was ordained in the Congregational Church, and served briefly as a parish minister in New Hampshire. By the end of the 1920s, however, he was back at Yale to do doctoral work in the New Testament. Impelled by a fascination with eschatology, that branch of theology concerned with "last things," he focused research and imagination on traditional themes: death, the end of the world, and the ultimate destiny of humanity. But this was no antiquarian theological interest; it was his way into a deeper understanding of the Gospel and the times in which he lived. It is not difficult to connect the academic study that culminated in *Eschatology and Ethics in the Teaching of Jesus* (1939, 1950, 1978) with the trauma of World War I; it is even easier to understand why throughout his career he was drawn to the apocalyptic literature of both Jews and Christians. In France he had been inside an apocalypse, had felt the earth reel and rock, had seen the foundations of the world laid bare (2 Sam. 22: 8, 16). It would not do to dismiss these biblical visions, as many did at the time, as surreal and grotesque fantasy; they were, he would argue, grounded in an actual Armageddon he had witnessed firsthand. "Reality" as it had been known before the world had been torn open for judgment. It was time for revelation.

The correspondence Wilder saw between ancient apocalyptic and the experience of his own generation—between notions of biblical crisis and the revolutions of the twentieth century—inspired an already established biblical scholar to become a literary critic as well. Turning to texts sacred and secular, ancient and modern, he discovered in them a common situation, what in a 1971 essay he called "nakedness to Being," an "immediacy to the dynamics of existence." When you live in a ruined world, you must study the ruins. Literature was a place to begin.

He began, in fact, with the particular literature of biblical writers: parable, myth, apocalypse, and Christian rhetoric in all its forms. Moreover, rather than travel the well-worn, dusty paths of the New Testament academy,

Wilder invested himself in an exploration of biblical imagination at a time (unlike the present day) when few were doing so. What precisely was the world the Scriptures asked us to enter, and how did language bring it to life? Parable and apocalyptic were especially compelling to him as they emerged, he argued, from "a crucible where the world is made and unmade."

Wilder did not approach the Bible "as literature," but rather as the Word of God articulated in a variety of literary forms. He welcomed the new attention being paid by literary scholars to the Scriptures—Northrop Frye, Robert Alter, Frank Kermode—and was grateful that windows had been opened "in an ancient library long obscured by stained glass and cobwebs" (as he wrote in an endorsement of Alter and Kermode's *Literary Guide to the Bible*). Yet he was not uncritical of what they found on the sacred page, nor did his interest in literary theory prevent him from arguing against the Deconstructionist notion that biblical narrative (*pace* Kermode's *The Genesis of Secrecy*) was finally indeterminate and open-ended. For Wilder, the Gospel of Mark, for instance, was "too urgent for puzzles and mystification"; it was not a cryptogram but an "opening and crowning disclosure" of glory.

In a daring move for a "guild" scholar, even one long drawn to questions of biblical interpretation, Wilder also opened his readers to the poetry, fiction, and drama of the twentieth century. An early foray into this career-long exploration was *The Spiritual Aspects of Modern Poetry* in 1940; a decade later came the decennial Bross Prize-winning *Modern Poetry and the Christian Tradition* (1952), *Theology and Modern Literature* (1958), and then *The New Voice: Religion, Literature, and Hermeneutics* (1969), where he touches on novelists (Proust, Gide, Sartre) and poets (Eliot, Robert Lowell, David Jones). These books invite the theological reader to be at once nourished and challenged by twentieth-century literature. However, the were written not only to expand the horizons of biblical scholars, but also to develop an interest in religion among those not inclined to seek it out. Still more ambitious is Wilder's 1976 book, *Theopoetic*, with its call for a renewal of biblical religion itself through the cultivation of the imagination. This required the risk of the new, stepping beyond the safety of the familiar and time-worn to explore deeper waters: "Old words do not reach across the new gulfs, and it is only in vision and oracle that we can chart the unknown and new-name the creatures." Before the message, came the vision; before the sermon, the hymn; before the prose, the poem. (He began his life as a writer in 1923, after all, as a Yale Younger Poet.)

Wilder's *The Bible and the Literary Critic*, published in 1991—just two years before his death in his 98th year—offers his own retrospection on a life's work spent on a border between Scripture and literature, proclamation and critique, God's Word and the poet's new account of everything old. Thanks to Wipf & Stock's republication of his works in "The Amos N. Wilder Library," we now have a chance not merely to look back on an extraordinarily varied creative life but to realize anew what it stands to offer our future explorations of the Bible and its literary afterlife.

Peter S. Hawkins
Professor of Religion and Literature
Yale Divinity School
New Haven, CT
October 2013

CONTENTS

Poetry and Roots: A Conversation with Margaret Rigg   7

Imagining the Real: A Comment on the Themes   29

From Amos . . .

    The Unmenaced Towers: Hadrian's Villa   37
    Logos   41
    Sunrise on the Himalayas   42
    Interlude   44
    Marriage of Minors   45
    Discord and Resolution   47

. . . and for him

    A Letter by Stanley R. Hopper   48
    A Poem for Amos Wilder
      by Arnold Kenseth   51

Wilderiana: Dates and Places   53

POETRY AND ROOTS

from a conversation with Margaret Rigg

AW: I brought along this poem, "The Unmenaced Towers: Hadrian's Villa," a very old one. You could use this one, if you want to, in the "Tome".

MR: Could you read it out loud?

AW: I could, yes.

MR: I like to *hear* a poem, to know a poem first by having it spoken, I seem to come in on it better, feel it clearer, when I can hear it read first. I seem to go back always to the idea of poetry being oral, that once people spoke in *that way* when human feelings were really heightened.

AW: Well, my point about this poem—although it's written years and years ago—was that one aspect of poetry that is everlastingly important is song (it's very much neglected today) and that while this poem is old-fashioned, it nevertheless ends in song, in singing, incantation—that's so much what poetry's *doing*.

MR: Song . . . as a celebration or as an asking?

AW: Song? Well, almost any kind of expression can take the form of song . . . can take a lyric aspect . . . isn't the earliest poetry rhythmic?

MR: Yes.

AW: It's like nature in that. Some of the oldest sacred texts we have are confessional, the ones dug up in Mesopotamia. The symbols also suggest that these formulas are very early, second millennium B.C. or before, magic and confessional, exclamations really but *nevertheless a chant quality about them.* It is true that there is a great deal of *good* contemporary poetry that has no song in it at all. Of course, they might say, "Well, it doesn't have song in the sense that Tennyson had song or that Keats had song," but they could claim that it has a different kind of musical quality. Sometimes one has to conclude that it's a poetry to be *read,* rather than to be heard, a great deal of it, and therefore, not first of all for oral chant or recitation. But, on the other hand, today we have the poetry readings in the coffeeshops that are oral. They often have rhythmic and incantatory appeal.

MR: I sometimes wonder if coffeeshop poems, readings, are not really a kind of contemporary version of the *work song.*

AW: Are they? Those were songs usually of gangs hauling on ropes or working on the levees . . .

MR: Yes, or the chopping of cotton or . . .

AW: A work song in *that* sense.

MR: A work song . . . But they *feel* their work is in these ghetto-dark places, all night long. What do these poems talk about?!

AW: Well, if the poems come right out of the economic sphere, that is, the business of making their living, making their bread and butter, and associations that go with that, in a factory or in domestic chores, that would make it a work song ... but, if they're singing in a cafe? I suppose that kind of singing always has a ceremonial aspect. Such work songs are not personal but liturgical. Their work rhythms rejoin the rhythms of nature.

MR: I think so. When we talked earlier, you mentioned "the masses..."

AW: I was talking about the *unknown American masses* and the grass roots and the fact that *no one knows their secrethood, their history, or their promise*. There's a deep American myth, or myths, in the making, gestating, which are often overlooked, or not sufficiently reverenced. I'm thinking of a certain fastidious school of critics who look only to New York and Greenwich Village for their best creative work. They don't recognize that out there among those "Philistines" there *may be something going on*, too. These critics are too deracinated, I feel they don't have roots in America, in that aspect of it. It doesn't mean their witness isn't important. I mean, they are talking about "alienation" in the city and so forth, and no doubt this is very important and it's international. But there is also the mysterious phenomenon of the great American public *out there*, you know, Kansas, Idaho, Arkansas, the "heartland." ...

One reason I'm interested is that my brother and Gertrude Stein found this of great common interest. What *is* an American? They talked about it, she wrote about it ...

MR: ... her book, *The Making of Americans* ...

AW: Of course, that's her own testimony, she looked on that as a kind of Bible of her own, reporting the experiences of her own forebears and family, the network of her family in the American grass roots and the underground of American society. She felt that was terribly important. She hated to be called an expatriate. She always thought of herself as an American, fascinated by what it was to be an American. And my brother and she had this in common.

Although he wasn't among that first group that went to Paris with Hemingway and Cummings and Dos Passos who knew her at that time, he knew her soon afterwards and later, when she came to Chicago and lectured at the University of Chicago. By that time they were very close friends. Their friendship was never broken as many of her friendships were. He thought she was a wonderful conversationalist. I think he was quite ready to say that much of her writing was difficult, but he valued many things she wrote and he valued her ideas. She was an idea-woman and she would often come out with a sudden flash of insight about this or that. She wasn't fooling people, she wasn't a charlatan.

But we were speaking of their interest in the American...

Our family was brought up in the middle west and we had a Maine background. My father was a kind of populist. He was the editor of a middle western newspaper, a popular speaker at county fairs. He was a great wit and humorist and remembered for all that. He made us all work on farms every summer. Thornton and I spent one whole summer on a farm in Vermont. He spent one summer on the farm of the Mt. Hermon School in Northfield, Massachusetts, and spent another long, hot summer on the Berea College farm in Kentucky. I spent a summer in Saratoga, California, picking apricots and prunes with a good old-fashioned farmer who never let us off one day in the summer except Sundays, religiously, and the Fourth of July.

MR: Oh, well, that's good!

AW: Another summer it was citrus fruits in southern California. Two summers I got away from it when I went to agricultural college. I went to the University of California School of Agriculture one summer. I learned how to bud and graft fruit trees, agronomy and so on. Another summer it was the University of Wisconsin, which has the most famous department of agriculture for dairying in the country, and I learned how to make ice cream and cheese there.

MR: Oh, did you learn how to make cheese!

AW: And I learned that when butter is made you put a little coloring in it because in some markets, they like it redder and in other markets they like it yellower. At one time I was able to judge horses, pigs, and cows. I could have gone to a fair, you know, and been a judge, at a county fair! Anyway, this suggests father's bucolic or rural convictions about what was important about educating American children. My sister was telling me yesterday, our father had her go to Battle Creek, Michigan. He also made her go to a horticultural institution in Pittsburgh, Pennsylvania. I know that my younger sister went to a Four-H school one summer.

MR: And during those years your father was out in China . . . what was he doing there?

AW: Well, he was a Consul General out there. He had become well-known in connection with what was called "Wisconsin Progressivism." This was in LaFollette days and the whole country was excited by what was being done in Wisconsin politics especially by Robert LaFollette, Sr. The University of Wisconsin social liberals, the sociology people, became very influential and my father, being the editor of the chief Republican paper in the capital, became known as an interpreter of what was going on in the state. All this led to my father's appointment as a consul in Hong Kong in 1906 by Theodore Roosevelt. We all went out and then he was moved to Shanghai later but lost his health. My father had interesting experiences in Shanghai at the time of the Chinese revolution there (1911). The Chinese leaders appreciated him because he had organized a Luncheon Club where Chinese merchants would be guests and members along with the French, American, British, and German business and diplomatic people. When my father left in 1914 the Club gave the family a beautiful silver set, with dragons all over it, which we still have.

Father's democratic sympathies *and* his belief in the common people made him afraid we would become eggheads. Of course, all of us did, Thornton and I, and my sisters! My sister Isabel wrote several novels and my sister Charlotte shared the Shelley Memorial Award in poetry with Ben Belitt one year. So we all *did* become eggheads—but nevertheless my father probably had inoculated us against certain forms of academic and aesthetic irresponsibility.

MR: Do you agree with that form of education now?

AW: It certainly went in one ear and out the other as far as any learning of how-to-do anything *practical* went. My wife will tell you how poor a help I am about the house or in the garden. But what I think *was* invaluable was the initiation into the dreams and hungers and travail of ordinary people.

MR: Because you *were* with certain kinds of people, working, that you wouldn't have been with otherwise.

AW: But it was also a question of values and responsibilities. Our father was always very suspicious of Bohemians as being triflers. When Thornton began to write, he said he was "carving cherry stones," a pleasant but trifling occupation. Our father, in Hong Kong, saw the Western diplomatic and social circles there over against the teeming millions of Chinese with the immense problems of the Far East, and the insensitivity to it on the part of many Western diplomats. So he had this serious concern that came out of his Puritan background. He was similarly suspicious of some aspects of academia.

MR: Too ivory towery . . . ?

AW: Playing games, you see . . . *in* the ivory tower. Playing games with the figures and with the letters and with the words and the ideas and being in a ghetto, shut away from the real world. A journalist, a conscientious journalist, a citizen with social responses would know. I think that was a good caution inbred in all of us. As my sister said the other night, at least we didn't *waste* our summers in Atlantic City or playing golf or playing bridge the way so many of our contemporaries did.

MR: Would your father talk with you after a summer and ask, "What did you learn . . .?", any sort of verbal testing, as to what it had meant to you?

AW: One reason it's hard to answer that is he was so far away. Our family was separated for years when we were growing up. It was a question of American schooling for the children. I never went back to China after the first six months, and when the other ones went back they weren't there very long.

MR: How old were you when you were in China?

AW: Eleven. But with my father, there was a running fire of letters to every one of us for years and years, with admonitions and inquisitions and affection and suggestions and warnings, all sorts of things. He was a very intensive parental planner for his children.

But our father's relation with education in China, also with the economic business in the Far East, meant that he took many American groups through China. One of the leading sociologists from the University of Wisconsin, E. A. Ross, dedicated his book, *The Changing Chinese*, to my father as "eloquent interpreter of the best Americanism." From my father *that* kind of social responsibility and international responsibility and concern about the common life undoubtedly influenced all of us. I stress it because some critics have pictured my father's Puritan influence on Thornton as harmful.

MR: Now, it occurs to me, Amos, that with this kind of

family *network*, to begin with, and then your own pursuits of study and teaching, that over the decades that you have lived you have been able to say: This decade . . . I saw the world *this* way, and *then* I couldn't see it that way any more, because of what had happened. Have you done that, do you think, or anything near it?

AW: Well, I think *anyone* who went to college, as I did, around the 1920's, lived through World War I and the Depression and all, must have registered a change in outlook. The big change for almost all of us was our reaction against Idealism and Romanticism, whether in art or in religion. With what we had gone through we were initiated into a new outlook and sensibility. This meant that we were prepared to appreciate all that is meant by modern literature and modern art. This change in my interests and sensibility is reflected in my book, *The Spiritual Aspects of the New Poetry*, 1940, which deals with Eliot, Jeffers, D. H. Lawrence, Yeats, Kenneth Patchen, etc., whom I had long been reading.

MR: Was this new outlook more humanized?

AW: I think that it was *always* deeply human, at least in our American tradition, but it was a *different* sense of the human. What does one make of the turn to abstraction in painting? Anyway, the human image became distorted in art. This was true also of poetry and the novel; they reflected the *same* influences that gave rise to cubism and surrealism. Berdyaev and Tillich both wrote books about what was happening to culture in the twenties *(The End of Our Age* by Berdyaev and Tillich's *The Religious Situation)* and they cited the work of painters of that time, Matisse, Picasso, and others, to suggest that the image of the human had become lost, distorted or tortured. Was *that* a movement toward humanism or not? I would say it was a *transition* from an inadequate understanding of man, of the image of man, to a richer, more profound sense of the dynamics of human nature. You had to break up the old simplistic representational idealism, break that up, before you could grasp a deeper humanism . . .

MR: To see more . . . In other words, in the visual arts there is a truism referred to in art history courses: "No one ever *saw* a sunset *before* Turner painted one." People, of course, *did* see the sunset, but when a painter showed it to us as art, then we made the meaning. Later came Picasso and others, showing us our brokenness. And we have learned that in brokenness also is meaning, human meaning. With our enlarged sensitivity we might see/feel and know what more there is to be seen, felt, known. Various artists and thinkers are our guides to the interiors.

AW: Yes. Or look at the new appeal of the masks from Africa, of what we call primitive art in Latin America and Africa, the masks and the grotesques and the forms of distortion of vision that appeared in non-Western art. These were not merely pursued by the European-American artists because they wanted to reject traditional art as they knew it, *but because they saw* in them a certain dynamic aspect of human nature and human reality which they thought was a positive witness they could make. Human nature has these deeper, dynamic elements which can often best be demonstrated by way of distortion and the grotesque. *Life is more volcanic than we thought it was!* And you can't represent it by the usual Easter lily or by a nice rural painting of a sunset on a farmhouse.

The interesting part of that is: What elements in our society accepted this revisioning of the world and how far did the response to modern art, or to the modern sense of reality, *penetrate* our world? And then that leads me to ask the question, what if I'm interested in middle America and in the mainstream in this culture and its problems and possibilities, beyond those of the Philistinism you usually associate with it? *How do I reconcile that interest with* this realization I have that there is some awareness which they haven't been educated to?

But another comment to make at this point is that the new movements in the arts, the new sense of reality that went with them, as always with movements and culture, soon could become a *fashion* and a *fad* and could become a *stereotype*. Inferior artists or imitative artists or faddist artists or exhibitionist artists can easily take up an important, new, and significant movement and exploit it for their own purposes, and since there are so few genuine artists of great stature, the potboilers and sensationalists can easily draw attention to their version of what's going on. So it seems to me that the critic or even the ordinary person interested in what is genuinely important often has difficulty in distinguishing between the authentic and the imitative or the spurious.

The new pathfinders, *they have hearts*. They pay a high price for their discoveries and their initiatives and for their new forms, their new work. They pay a price in deep personal discipline and travail. They also pay a price in loneliness and in following their own unpopular idiom and vision. Certainly this has been true of those great pathfinders and iconoclasts who have changed our vision of "reality" and shaped what we call "the modern."

But I myself think that what we call "modernism" has reached an end point and that there's a new beginning due, *which will link it up with the older continuities* (which for the time being were by-passed). Any revolutionary movement inevitably tends to discard some important things along with those things that it properly and understandably rejects. Following its own new vision it is almost inevitably bound to lose contact with the deepest continuities in human life. Therefore, the time comes when this particular experiment— it may be an experiment that lasts a hundred years—the time comes when this particular experiment needs to *go back to its roots* and to the roots of all creative impulse.

MR: Needs to get fed again . . .

AW: Yes, and nourished again . . . perhaps be immersed in that, what Walt Whitman would call grass (not *that* kind of grass!), the leaves of grass, you see, *ordinary* leaves of grass. I take it that in your *Survivor's Box*, Peg, you've got some witnesses to what I'm talking about. That is one most important thing about the Black arts, for instance. It's a kind of re-baptism in a human experience which is older and *anterior* and represents a sense of basic human continuity.

MR: I think so, I feel it that way. I hope it is that way. They remind us, the human root is a *shared* one. We *share* this *human root*.

AW: And where that sharing is found between two branches otherwise separate, and so far separated, it must be pretty fundamental and pretty deep.

MR: Yes! And as Wolfe has Ben say in *Look Homeward Angel:* "Sometimes you have to go a very long way out of your way to come back the right way." I think of his meaning that . . . often one has to take the trouble to find the root connections . . . really attend to those deeper significations . . . in a sense, to "lead" us all through, to higher ground . . .

AW: Now when the French painters went to the South Sea islands, when they went to primitive art for re-invigoration, there would be something of the same rediscovery of the basic, the deeper root.

MR: But in writing the poetry that you've written and in dealing with theology the way you have for many years, if you had to say *what* it all is really *centered around* or *directed toward*, could you possibly put that in a few words or a sentence?

AW: Inevitably, I'm old-fashioned in the sense that my initial orienting vision of things came out of the Biblical shaping, the roots and personal experience, at that time in life, you know, when you're seventeen or eighteen or twenty-five when these things are pretty irreversible. They shape your outlook, your categories, your further experience. That was determinative for me in any case. But *always*, this anchorage in tradition was unhappy unless it could establish *humanist relationships* of all kinds: with the classics, with art and literature, with nature and the love of nature. It was, therefore, in this sense, non-dogmatic or open, and looking for enrichment from sources that were not part of the conventional piety or orthodoxy of the time. Thus my first concern with poetry when I was a young minister was that I found the people in the churches—in seminaries too, the teachers as well as the clergy—I found them limited in their responsiveness to whole domains of significance: aesthetics, nature, European culture (I could have added Far Eastern culture if I had then known more about that). These were not part of the picture.

MR: Where did Americans, if we go back to Gertrude Stein and Thornton Wilder, get their interest in *what it is to be an American?* Now, where did Americans get the impetus for aesthetics on a *useful* high plane?

AW: The interest of Stein and my brother was not first of all in some specifically American aesthetic. It was in the potential for it and the different kind of human breed which had these different possibilities coming out of Europe.

MR: Informed by Thoreau?

AW: The contrast is with the closed societies of Europe, in which a person often lived in the same house in which his parents and grandparents had lived, and in which social mobility was so limited for a thousand years. That kind of society produces a kind of bell-jar culture and human type. America had these endless geographic horizons, the mobility, the migration of these European peoples to America with the experience of the frontier and the loss of roots from Europe, and then the loss of roots from the East to the West coast. All that made a different kind of human being. This is the kind of thing that Thornton and Gertrude Stein would earnestly talk about and then its implication for art. Then they would turn to Walt Whitman and my brother would quote a passage from Walt Whitman which ran something like this: "Is there any classic of ancient Greece, Roman, or European background which is in vibration, so to speak, with democracy as American society knows it or is not even an insult to it?" Much of the great art of the past came out of *elitist societies* and so its "vibes" are out of tune with what's possible in the art of a people in which democracy is partially realized. My brother would talk in terms of *potential*. The great and distinctive arts of America are in gestation; so he would talk of new images, new myths, new arts. And the dreams and myths of the New World will always be *political* and not *psychological* like those of modern Europe. It's very fashionable for our modern critics in literary and artistic circles to talk about Walt Whitman, praise him . . .

MR: and Thoreau and Ruskin . . .

AW: They usually mean, first of all, that Walt Whitman invented a new kind of verse, or they mean that Walt Whitman declared our independence from Europe, but they don't mean what Whitman was *mainly* talking about, his vision of *democracy*. That's lost sight of. Do they really believe in it? Do they believe in Missouri and Arkansas and so on, and their potential as a source of new myths and of new creative possibilities? They are still too concerned with Nietzsche and Rimbaud and Baudelaire and the expatriates. I think Ezra Pound, however mixed up he was, carried over something of our American grass-roots moral and political concern. Speaking of *the real meaning of art,* he said that *it provides human beings with the incentives to go on living!* You can't get more fundamental than that. That's a way of talking about the moral values in art *without being moralistic.* Art has to to with *life,* and the springs and incentives of living.

MR: Do you know Suzanne Langer?

AW: Well, I know some of her writings.

MR: Her *Philosophy in a New Key* is so crucial for my understanding of what's going on.

AW: Yes, I read it long ago and it was to me a very enlightening book, a very thrilling book. It has to do with imagination as well as with reason in life and art. Remind me of what struck you.

MR: Where she talks about, mostly in music, about *creativity* (but "music" translates into the visual arts and all the other arts for me) she talks about . . . one instance I remember very clearly and go back to: Somebody on a street corner is in pain. All the person in pain knows to do is just *scream* on that street corner and people pass by and feel: *"That* person's having a problem." But an artist takes the very same feeling and will write a poem that finds certain words to let other people come through the same proscenium *into the experience* and not confuse it with their own life. It's "out there," *I'm* "here," it's similar and they can do a *translation.* That's the difference between photo-journalism and fine art.

AW: She relates art to *what is of significance,* to the real experience. In a valid way. No one could say that this is moralistic or that this is a utilitarian view of art.

MR: Right, right, right, *right!* And the other thing that *feeds* me, continually, is Denis de Rougemont's essay in the book, *Spiritual Problems in Contemporary Literature.* He says, "a stone or stick carved or painted in a certain way once carried a *meaning,* a life and death meaning, and was *useful;*

whereas for us, how to get there faster, for whatever reason, is useful (!) . . . (and therefore more meaningful"!) Langer shows a complete vacuum between there and here, and she taught us to come back to *organic* understandings.

AW: That's one of the main themes of my little book, *Theopoetic*. It's a matter of *reversing the process of disenchantment*, since the modern secular world has become disenchanted. The modern world has *lost the sense of the sacred*. We forfeit the imaginative dimension.

MR: . . . which is *risk!* Our no risk-taking . . .

AW: The loss of the magic sense of reality. Now what we're in for today is a *recovery* of that. It appears in many forms, it appeared in the hippies in a very preliminary way, an important way, but nevertheless not so important as what was *behind* it, which was much more general. This shift of sensibility is manifest today in many quarters and that's why Berdyaev long ago said *we're moving toward a new middle ages*, a new age of faith in *that* sense. He didn't mean a new middle ages in the sense of obscurantism or superstition. He meant that the modern secular world was moving toward a new epoch in which there would be a more general awareness of the mysterious and the *unpredictable* in all aspects of life.

MR: Breaking through!

AW: It *is* a breaking through in many ways. It can have questionable aspects, for example in the churches. It can take on many obscurantist and mistaken forms both in the churches and outside of them, but it can also have creative and promising outcomes. How does one assess the evangelical movement? The Adventists and Pentecostals are growing in numbers. What about prayer breakfasts and the audiences of Billy Graham? But then there is the interest in flying saucers and astrology and extrasensory perception! Look at the bookstores today under "religion." One has many-sided testimony to the fact that there's a kind of groundswell interest in mysticism and the prerational and the non-secular dimension of life. It may be superstition and the false occult, but behind it all there is no doubt a revolt against "one-dimensional man" and a hunger for some sort of transcendence and free creativity.

MR: If a powerful movement—political or not—is under way, if it gets *cut off* prematurely . . . it seems to return later, very often in some rather distorted form. The rise of "Hitler Germany" and then the smashing of it did not *end* the *idea*, which seems to have gone underground and returned later, outside Germany, as if the idea "seed" grows again, this new time in a vacuum created by the former massive denial—the cutting-off . . . it seems to me that history gives us many sorts of examples of a human idea going *on*, cropping up later in a distorted form . . . distorted from its earlier manifestation, since the *idea* could not live out its whole life-form before, "naturally" to *its* organic end . . . and I keep puzzling over that view of human history and wondering about it.

AW: What you're saying is: there is a groundswell, a new movement of creative possibility and realization going on *which was frustrated at a certain point* and *now* we see various species or pseudo-forms of that *frustrated* creativity appearing in various ways. That's the "only way it can get out." Or "go on," so to speak.

MR: I symbolize that to myself as being like a *broken* network. When the net is torn and some fish (that you want to catch) get *out* but other fish (which you may not want to catch) get *in* . . . so now the "catching" itself is changed because of the tear in the wholeness of the net and you have a *new* mix. A new configuration *now* begins to occur. And this "new" does not just get "grafted on" to that *same* old root. Therefore it's as if the organic fullness continues on, in a distorted way, in the historical continuum. Of course, perhaps, the tear itself, which allowed the new *mix* of fish, was (is) *the* distortion!

AW: Are you speaking of what's actually happened in art itself as well?

MR: I'm speaking there of the sociological aspect. For instance, the sociological aspect of, say, the American dollar, which is often thought of as "replacing" creativity or any need to be personally creative, personally accountable. Some Americans think it is possible to go to the local stores and *buy* creativity and don't really *need* to locate the source of creativity in the self, or, even *know* some other or others who can and do create. Americans now seem to have "the mind-set" for going out and *buying* . . . whatever . . . an art object, an art experience (a concert or play or ballet), and even a machine that can be programmed to "do it for us" and all we have to do is come to some place for getting that sort of thing with enough money to buy it. It also seems to me that the *selective* eye (in each American) thus is being less trained and so more dependent upon "those experts out there" to select *what* shall be processed to us, to advertize it to us and then market it widely. It's "business" . . . the "art" of selling. And after awhile, we the buyers of culture (of the thoughts and the arts) become very dim-eyed or even blind . . . not even performing as "good" buyers, the "market" then, dries up . . . a return to the "barbaric".

But a culture that is doing *more* than merely *funding* creativity, so that "it" can go on, for whatever purpose is a culture which ORGANICALLY *is creative in* each individual locally. *I* can then meet, talk with, exchange views with, get to know an artist, not from New York City but right here where I am living and working . . . and further, I can then *see* my own relationship to the creativity going on, I myself can help fund it, attend it (performances, exhibitions, publications) and not only "help it live and grow" but have a "say" in its development. That is, I can see and feel and assess my own in-put which goes to make the art work. I can then, in this way keep art honest . . . related to *my* living life and *my (our)* concerns and the very building of *our* human culture . . . *at* the grass-roots.

To go now, as we do, in response to some advertisement we see in a newspaper or magazine or book, to a department store and buy a "piece" of work (art work)—or to a concert hall to "buy" a piece of musical experience—*means: that we never* even get *near* "*art*", whatever *that* is . . . since we never take the opportunity to nurture in ourselves any bit of sense of the creative *process*. Rather, we Americans have already efficiently "chopped-off" our lives from many creative roots, and are eager to be told that we can "just as effectively" "support" art—in our culture—when we have the money and use some of it to *buy art*, or whatever we are *told* (taught) *is* art. I think in this way exactly a people gets DEhumanized. I see evidences of this dehumanization of me, of us, wherever I look, in the whole fabric of the American culture, not just in the "art-scene." This crucial chopping, a *making* of DISconnection, so that it is awfully late to try and reach toward a culture of wholeness and health, and we each have so very little to *feed* on . . . so little that is organic, to nourish us. Rather a drastic time and place for the USA-American "culture." Yes, BUT what do we do?

AW: *Well, then one has to start over, one has to look for new beginnings, here and there, a new more authentic network of relationships* and they have to make their way through lack of recognition for awhile and *it's a question of health against disease*. I think if one moves to the sociological and political realm one could find examples. I would agree with what you're saying there. This disconnectedness goes with a sense of emptiness and thing-ness. That's what the plays of Ionesco are about, the loss of meaning in general. Genuine human relations and the authentic sap of organic life and growth are excluded.

MR: I want to go to *your own writing of poetry*. When you write poetry . . . well, we could talk about your choosing a theme *or if it chooses you* and becomes something you want to write about and do write about. But the theme itself: *choosing words. How* do you do that organically, how do *you* make the word choice?

AW: There are two levels: some words are *given* to you and then, after that, there's a process of completing the poem and then there is more conscious attention to the words you choose and the words you reject. In that aspect in which they are given to you, the words are *part of* the intense mood in which some expression comes. It just naturally "erupts" and then you've got a good part of the poem given to you or initiated in that way. There may then be some conscious activity, however, involved in keeping hold of the original moment of epiphany or vision—what started you writing in the first place—so that what you have there won't be out of tune with what was originally given. So it's hard to say whether the visionary grasp came first or the language because they're *inseparable* from each other, the material and the total pattern. I've read lately some unpublished poems of Tony Stoneburner. Do you know Tony?

MR: Oh, yes!

AW: He's a very good friend of mine. He's down in Maine in the summer. He won the Hapwood Poetry Prize at the University of Michigan when he was a student there.

MR: I published him a lot in *motive*.

AW: In discussing poetry with him, I said, my test of a poem is double: *one*, whether it's got any *song* to it; *second*, it should have *unity*. Poems should be tied together so that they end somewhere related organically to where they began.

MR: Make some kind of pattern . . .

AW: They make a pattern. And there are no loose ends, and this applies not only to what you're writing *about* but also to the way it's written, to tones as well as to words. The great poems all have unity in the sense that there's enough imaginative force to shape a unity, to fuse them as metal is fused instead of having its alloys still showing.

MR: Yes! Yes!

AW: So that there must be *energy*, intensity behind the creative work if it is to be very significant or if it is to say anything new or if it is to put anything old together with anything new. *There has to be energy*, it has to have a high temperature, so to speak, to *fuse* it into a something that is really creative.

MR: Do you know Muriel Rukeyser?

AW: I've met her in the past. I remember her book about U.S. Rt. 1 from Maine to Florida, especially the part concerned with miners and lung disease. What an admirable testimony that was. But the most wonderful verse of hers that I know is a poem about John Brown which I've often quoted.

MR: I have her tape reading poetry . . . a tape that Alan Austin (who used to work for *motive* and is now editor of *Black Box*) produces for Open Classroom . . . You subscribe and it comes, two cassette tapes, so you have four sides, four times per year—expensive but quite good and it's poets saying their own poems, I'm really hipped on that, so I like it. But *I'd never heard of her before I heard this tape* and then I began asking literary people that I know about her. Somebody sent me her latest book, *Breaking Open*. She is powerful!

AW: Oh, well, I'll certainly get it and read it. Her poem, "The Soul and Body of John Brown," illustrates the point I was making earlier about America's political mythology and the promise of a native American literature and art . . .

IMAGINING THE REAL

IMAGINING THE REAL
A Comment on the Themes

It is with this caption of "imagining the real" that I would like to embroider some of the themes in the foregoing conversation, also in connection with my own writing, some examples of which appear later.

Margaret Rigg and I began with our common commitment to the imagination, as it bears not only on poetry and art but on all life and experience. Our concern with the "roots" of poetry and art was not meant to be defensive about any and all tradition. We were thinking partly about the alienation of art and the artist through commercialization and marketing. We were also thinking about how even great schools in art and great traditions in symbol and liturgy can in the course of time diverge from where life is lived.

Thus our slogan, "imagining the real," challenges some kinds of aestheticism. It also conceals surprises.

Some, for example, would not want creativity and the imagination tied down to anything, whether roots or reality!

Their prescription, rather, is: explore the *novum!* Break the molds! Improvise and liberate! Put out to sea from all shores without cargo. Emptiness has its own inebriation. Imagine the non-human! Here is the true fabulation.

What after all is the "real"? Pedestrian facts, prosaic tedium and the bondage of the actual? Surely, they would say, some leap into the surreal is to be preferred. Or is the "real" some Platonic or Victorian idea of the Good, the True and the Beautiful that has long been found to be banal, bourgeois and sentimental.

No. When *we* speak of imagining the real we mean that the modern artist and seer should, first, stay within the human, and, second, wrestle with all the givens and social bonds of our creaturely state. Imagination means, certainly, the transmutation of circumstance, but not disengagement or aestheticism or false spirituality.

Whether in art or religion much today scants, short-cuts, aspects of the real. Gaps between language (or other media) and life are not bridged. Even what may once have been integral and authentic does not strike home to where we live. The acoustics have changed. Besides that, the situation is highly pluralistic; we belong to many differing cultural and spiritual families and traditions, each of which has its own links with the real and its own distortions.

Therefore Peg Rigg calls for the "organic" and the "incarnational." Like the work-song, any work of art should have an essential relation to our elemental activities and relationships. Or, more largely, the works of the mind and the imagination should be responsive to generic human needs and potentials, and nourish these. This emphasis accounts for the large place that ecological concerns, the arts of minority groups, social causes and the forgotten graces and talents of obscure generations have in her *Survivors Box*. True cultural creativity and visionary incitement are far more widely diffused than we would suppose if we confine ourselves to academies, museums, galleries and the media.

No doubt it can be objected that a society depends upon its great artists, ultimately well-publicized, and their succession for its visioning and re-visioning of reality. In this light the input of such modest witnesses as those we have pointed to can seem unimportant. But there are several things that can be said on this point. "To have great poets we must have great audiences also." More important, even the reigning figures and their horizons of vision, their schools and their sensibility, are continually open to challenge and revision. Even with their mastery they are often mirrors of the spirit of an age, and older or newer perspectives and strategies claim attention. New impulses and voices arise precisely out of the common life and its deeper dramas and urgencies. The scenarios of the public imagination are ever changing. They can also be deepened and purified. Such revolution of images is often traced to obscure beginnings and to the probity and discipline of unknown artists nourished at the roots of their community.

In our conversation one theme of my own is related to these considerations. I speak there of the grass-roots American potential, whose artistic and spiritual resources seem to me to be underestimated by modern critics. It is a question of honoring buried roots and hidden archetypes. Can any good come out of Main Street? Is there some momentous promise still in our homespun or garish public? Do we have to make this distinction still between the cultured and uncultured, the elite and the masses, the sophisticated and the common, the highbrow and lowbrow?

In Europe even after the industrial revolution there has always been the class distinction between the elites and "*le people*" (or, the proletariat). But with us "the people" is not at all the same thing as *"le peuple"* in its disparaging sense. The ordinary American, the common citizen, the man in the street, is not hereditarily disposed or resigned to a class status or station in life, or to a fixed cultural pattern received from the past or his betters. It is true that we have our Philistines or Babbits, but they are found in all conditions.

It is true that in many aspects of town and country and suburb—in Middle America if we know what that means—we do not find certain visible artistic accomplishments and activities that are cherished in our cities and colleges and universities. But we must look deeper. The mobility is there in this sense also, that is, the continuity and interpenetration. Many of our best artists, moreover, come from the grass roots and are nourished by its vitality and independence, however much their mature work takes on cosmopolitan character.

More important are the distinctive New World motifs and legacies which operate in the society as a whole, and which have not come to full expression in our period as they have at times in the past. This is what I referred to in speaking of the myth which is gestating in the New World, a unique vision related to our beginnings, and one operative in a hidden way throughout the whole population.

In his book, *American Renaissance*, F. O. Matthiessen spoke of the "still undiminished resources" of that legacy exploited by our classic American writers. Herman Melville praised in Hawthorne "that unshackled democratic spirit of Christianity in all things." Matthiessen saw it as still determinative for the promise of America. Perhaps one could say that this creativity arises out of a tension between Calvinism and our New World empiricism, our secular democratic spirit of insubordination. In any case, where many who look from abroad see only a wasteland of Philistia in Middle America—materialism, chauvinism, bigotry—we should look deeper.

The way to cure the corruptions of the American dream is to mine it more deeply for its creative potential. This lies especially in its transcendental vision of brotherhood.

This invocation of the past is not to be understood as a defense of Calvinist dogma. Yet America's secular and pluralist experience owes much in terms of depth to its biblical archetypes. The moral polarities and emotional gamut of Milton and Bunyan carried over into the ethos of our people. It is this stamp which sets limits to our betrayals of democracy. In this setting also, as I have suggested, the subjectivism and psychologism which characterize European modernism and post-modernism find an uncongenial soil. Nor need the arts and ikons of this vision be parochial. They can enter into fertilizing exchange with all human fabulation, East or West, especially where this is related to the affirmation of human dignity and the fashioning of a true community.

Finally, with respect to my own writing, I can link up our theme of "imagining the real" with certain of my preoccupations. My early interest in modern poetry reflected a discovery, as I have indicated in the conversation, that new aspects of the "real" were opened up after WW I, to those of my generation. At the same time I was always concerned to discriminate among modern voices and to "test the spirits." I read a great deal of contemporary French literature in the twenties, and learned to distinguish between great transcriptions of human experience as in Proust and Gide, and works of a more fateful moral and vertical dimension as in Peguy, Claudel and Mauriac. Abroad and at home I learned to appreciate the varieties of cultures and sub-cultures, the relativity of the arts and of pieties to their settings, and so to value both orthodoxies and heresies, traditions and revolts, both sophistication and naivete.

My experience in WW I initiated me into dimensions of

the imagination which have made much of life and letters seem insipid by comparison, but which confirmed for me the authority of the classics, and above all, the Scriptures. Any who read the poems in my first book of verse, *Battle-Retrospect*, published in the Yale Series of Younger Poets, may well be scandalized by the nostalgia there expressed. They should recognize that the drama of taking part in world-shaping events has its own repercussions. In any case, imagining the real could never thereafter be satisfied with what most modern classics or iconoclasts could view as important.

My poetry was always for me a kind of precipitate of experience, cherished rather as record than as art-work. Those chosen here may have the value of illustrating themes in the conversation especially with respect to changing views of the real.

"The Unmenaced Towers: Hadrian's Villa" and "Sunrise in the Himalayas" reflect the emphasis on the poet as singer, no doubt in both cases in a traditional mode. This kind of singing had to do with the prestige of historic places, shrines and figures. Our generation was often lyric about such topics, excited as here by themes of mutability and a tension between time and eternity. My earliest verse was "inspired" by a combination of the Platonic and the Christian, as in my poem, "Logos" here included, which was published in one of the best of the little magazines, *The Double Dealer* (New Orleans), in 1926.

"Interlude," written soon after my WW I experience as ambulance driver and combatant in the Field Artillery, will convey something of the apocalyptic overtones of battle. For this reason I was able to make use of it in an article, "The Rhetoric of Ancient and Modern Apocalyptic," published in *Interpretation*, 1971.

"Marriage of Minors" reports an experience during my village pastorate in New Hampshire in the late twenties. The use of free verse and colloquial detail in a religious poem helps to give it force. Yet such poems will inevitably appear sentimental unless the assumptions can be accepted. Poets and artists who work in a traditional vein should seek to be emotionally honest, but they have every right to work their own vein and speak their own kind.

"Discord and Resolution" represents a melding of lines from Hölderlin (specially appealed to by Heidegger) with my own additions.

The recent wave of interest in language and its structures and "how it works" has been important to me both in my biblical study and in my literary pursuits. Communication in any art or liturgy depends on social conventions, audience expectations, acoustics, apperception. In the arts this means especially symbols and dramatizations, but also shapes and forms. In the Bible this has drawn our attention particularly to the importance of the story and the metaphor. All this bears on the dynamics of speech and the plastic arts.

The real requires more than representation and calls for evocation, divination and enactment. Customary vision must be shocked by distortion, paradox, invention and by old and potent mythologies. Many of us learned these things from primitive art and speech, from such post-Bultmannians as Ernst Fuchs, from the hermeneutic consultations organized by Stanley Hopper and from the concerns of the structuralists. These kinds of tools and keys I sought to use in my books, *The New Voice* (1969), *Early Christian Rhetoric* (1964, 1971) and *Theopoetic* (1976).

Before the message, the vision...

ANW '76

THE UNMENACED TOWERS
Hadrian's Villa, Tivoli

Lavender fumes from sunset's dying torch
    Mantle the heaven,
The paling panels of night's western porch
    So lately riven
With crimson flares no longer flame and scorch
    With glowing levin.

The torch is quenched that cast its ruddy flare
    O'er the Campagna,
The hosts are vanished and the golden stair,
    Trump and hosanna,
The Sabines lose their flush, the dusky air
    Welcomes Urania.

Fold upon fold of somber loveliness
    Billowing and drifting
The gray cloud-masses ever eastward press
    Funnelling and rifting,
Ash from the sunset's smouldering wilderness
    Blowing and sifting;

And all that glory but a silhouette:
    The Villa Hadrian
An acropolis of cypresses like jet
    Against the meridian,
Its ruins gulfed even as its past is set
    Deep in oblivion.

The night has fallen on the glowing stone,
    The April color,
The Night has fallen on scepter and on throne
    Bright as no fuller
On earth can bleach, and past and present own
    The great Annuller.

An hour ago upon the mosaic'd floor
  Reft of its ceiling
I stood and watched the floods of daylight pour
  Luminous, revealing
Grove-secrets and crypt-mysteries; now no more:
  Day's ocean stealing

To other scenes, the ocean of the night
  Of equal power
Or greater to bring mystery to light
  Brings forth new dower
Of intimations in the identical site
  In the changed hour.

So intimations swarm upon the husk
  Of ancient splendors;
Read in the altered light of history's dusk
  A spirit tenders
More hallowed moods, breathing a fainter musk
  And dreams more tender.

For years distil the eternal from the days
  And leave to silence
All that once raged in time's advancing blaze
  Of lust and violence;
This quiet column marks their holier ways,
  The rest is silence.

Amid the imperial revelry and waste
  And mean appraisal
Of mortal things, this broken tablet chased
  By unknown chisel
With timeless beauty witnesses there paced
  Mid the carousal

Hearts that were bent in those forgotten fetes
  On deeply probing
The granite destinies, the marble fates,
  And on disrobing

*That Beauty whose heart therein palpitates,
   The dust ennobling.*

*The holier instincts floating in the mind,
   The prophet-hauntings,
Of peoples and of ages, undefined
   (While all the flauntings
And vanities to erasure are assigned
   And all the vauntings*

*Written on water), on the adamant
   Of earth are printed:
Awe stamps itself on granite, selfless want
   And faith are dinted
On the enduring stone, truth lives extant
   Durably minted.*

*The basalt and the porphyry may rift,
   The alabaster
Hewn from the core of earth may dust and sift
   And Vulcan's masters
The elements in their economy swift
   Hasten disaster*

*To all the marble parchments of the race,
   Annihilating
Token and tale of long departed grace,
   Ruthlessly fating
Earth's elder sanctities to want all trace
   And all relating.*

*Yet in the unthreatened bronze of ideal form
   Immune to fire,
Yet in the eternal ground, immune to storm
   And battle ire,
The adamant of thought, fixed, uniform,
   Each dim desire*

*Of earth's least daring, skilless worshipper
   Is carved forever*

In print of beauty exquisitely fair,
    The frail endeavor
Of dreams has built unmenaced temples there
    Effaced never.

A world there is whose fabrics never fall
    Nor bastions crumble,
Time breathes not there on parapet or wall,
    Nor thunders rumble
In the serene, nor meteors appal
    Nor tremors humble.

Without its wall from age to halcyon age
    No foes assemble,
The generations leave no heritage
    That man should tremble
Of feud or discord, and no hatreds rage
    Nor lusts dissemble.

I saw it mirrored in the lands of sleep:
    Slowly 'twas building.
The windless realms of fancy charmed it deep
    In light bewildering,
And from its pinnacles I saw flashes leap,
    Fires from their gilding.

                                           Tivoli, April 1922.

LOGOS

*The signature of mind is on the deep
And thought has sunk its seal upon the inane,
And sudden fancies made incursion on sleep,
And flashes lightened o'er the Night's domain.
Eternity shall hold the print of dreams;
Their subtle webs and filaments shall lie
Frozen in breathless climates in the seams
Of nature like some lost fern's gossamer die.
Form in the adamantine bastions, form!
Form in the crystal sphere, the triple bronze,
Form out of naught, to outlive with type and norm
Time's crawling insect-hill that slaves and spawns.
The soul is stamped on some Atlantian range
And silence chambers it above all change.*

Arachne: Poems. Yale University Press, 1928.

SUNRISE ON THE HIMALAYAS
From Tiger Hill

*Snows in the night loom in the sullen north
Beyond an abyss of ridges brimmed with cloud;
Now fade in night's diaphanous eclipse,
And now loom forth
Out of the darkness' fluctuating shroud,
Conscious e'er night has run
Of visitings from the unannounced sun.*

*For these sublime existences ignore
The traffickings of India's darkling floor
And human lore,
And speak each other, beaconing afar
To sun and star
In speech untaught,
And hold a converse far above our thought.
Their language like an undulation leaps
Across heaven's steeps
And laps the headlands of the day and night
With storms of light.*

*Upon those faces vast
Invisible beams in night's obscurity
Break into milky radiancy;
Their congregate white fires of the past;
The riotous stars have cast
Their silver illustrations on the height
And made the range their glaring satellite.*

*And like an alien mass
Beyond the confines of our heaving world,
Remote on seas of vapour wide unfurled
As the first shadows pass
And the first pallors of the dawn appear
It floats and overlooks the landscapes of our sphere.*

Whiter its chalky facets glow,
Sharper the granite fences show
Under night's paling lamps;
The continental slopes pitch high
Into mid-heaven their jagged ramps,
The lunar cirques and craters lie
Under an irised sky.

Now through the eastern murk the sun
Breaks with his sultry rim
And unto him
Earth tilts its nebulous floor
Till more and more
The auroral couriers run
To lend yon cosmic battlements their crimson benison.

And lucid morning follows in their train;
Day's diamond beam
Like some crystalline inundation brims
The heaven's rims:
The wide inane
Glitters, and bathes the world as in some luminous dream.

The aerial snows indue
A silvery hue;
Metallic glamors fleet upon the slopes.
The spirit gropes
In nameless visions and inhuman tracts
Beyond earth's calms and storms,
The eyeballs seared and blind
With gazing on the eternal cataracts
Of light that pour upon the world of forms
From the exhaustless fountains of eternal mind.

    Arachne: Poems. Yale University Press, 1928.

INTERLUDE (W.W.I)

Comrades, we bring this chapter to a close,
This long parenthesis of cosmic strife,
This interlude, touched with the grandiose,
Set in the uneventful tale of life.

For then this human swathe, this bandaging
That muffles us from the sublime was nigh
Threadbare with taking part in, witnessing
Too closely God's fate-laden strategy.

There we marched out on haunted battle-ground,
There smelled the strife of gods, were brushed against
By higher beings, and were wrapped around
With passions not of earth, all dimly sensed.

There saw we daemons fighting in the sky
And battles in aerial mirage,
The feverish Véry lights proclaimed them by,
Their tramplings woke out panting, fierce barrage.

Their tide of battle, hither, thither driven,
And we the shadows of celestial foes.
Filled earth and sky with cataclysmic throes,
Our strife was but the mimicry of heaven's

> Battle-Retrospect and Other Poems.
> Yale University Press, 1923.

MARRIAGE OF MINORS

Brother and sister in this world's poor family,
Jack and Jill out of this gypsy camp of an earth,
Here is where the injustice is greatest
And you feel it obscurely,
And you have a right to storm within yourselves
And seek sanctuary in one another's shabbiness.

This boy and this girl with all their abandonments and futility,
Folly and dereliction,
Whirled from ignominy to ignominy,
Condemned to all the wretched chores of the community—
O tribute of forlorn humanity!
Come for his benediction whom they have blasphemed,
And somehow sense that they touch—what?
God, the Higher, all that they have missed:
Innocence and mercy and compassion.

Poor lad, scourged from humiliation to humiliation,
Pressed by dirt and danger, squalor and exhaustion,
And bred on blasphemy and the poison of men's bitter spirit,
And the maudline imaginations of their lust;
Where else could it end but in this make-shift marriage?
And well may you storm within yourself, at the same time that
        you feel the awe of it.
God and the devil both have a hand in joining you,
And you are hardly at fault.

Poor sister in our earth's poor family,
Stupid and stupified and hallowed all at once,
Poor creature of poor moments,
Disinherited Eve,
How else could it come out but in this tumble at the first assault,
And yet God has put his finger on even this.

No bridesmaids nor flowers for you,
The groom hasn't given you these.

You came in an old coat.
One of the gang is best man and witness.
The boy minister goes through with it,
And there is no shower as you go out.
The sleigh waits outside in the heavy snowfall.
It is movie night in the village, and no one is about to spy you
    at the parsonage,
And so you go off in the blizzard to the lumber camps.
This is all the world gives you.

But the Son of Man of the wedding feast haunts such occasions
    and understands you.
He can turn the water into wine and such shame and loss into gain
In some world some time.

Lucy Hanks bore Nancy seven years before her marriage feast.
The Son of Man knows too well what the hells are, and the dumb
    wonderings and sicknesses of the soul,
And he is the only one who does know.
So endure these gusts and whirlwinds of the night until the
    morning breaks.

I heard the organ roll behind the snowfall and saw in it the con-
    fetti of the heavenly bridechamber,
Glimpsed the sons of the bridechamber rejoicing
In that City which is full of boys and girls playing in the
    streets thereof,
Before the Father whose face the angels of little children do
    always behold.

                        The Healing of the Waters: Poems.
                        Harper & Brothers, 1943.

DISCORD AND RESOLUTION

As in a snowfall
the vesper bells
that call men from the fields
to the evening meal
come dissonant and muted,
their changes
jumbled in the swarming dusk;

As through a swirling fog
the dead clangs of the bell-buoy,
swinging to the surges,
reach us muffled and awry,
deranged in the smother;

so the tolling of being
is damped and untuned,
the chime of creation
and the diapason of the heart
jangled by a swarm,
a fate, of lesser things

until again the true pitch
is sounded
for the clamor of the angelic choirs
and we hear the well-tempered accords
at the birth of the child,
as when the morning stars sang together
and all the sons of God shouted for joy.

Christianity & Crisis
December 25, 1972

(From a poem-letter of Stanley Hopper to Amos
Wilder, 1975—referring to Wilder's
dedication of his book of poems, *Grace
Confounding*, 1972, to Stanley Hopper
along with Nathan Scott. This poem includes
allusion to a number of Wilder's poems.)

Dear Amos:

Your poems I have read now
many times

> *and I have waited*
> *for the breeze to blow*
> *for some wild note*
> *from Orpheus' broken head*
> *to bound across the waters*
> *or for some stray cicada*
> *flaunting in the wind*
> *to light upon my hapless lyre*
> *and harmonize my scattered thoughts . . .*

> *or better yet*
> *to hope that Pegasus,*
> *that darling of the Muse,*
> *when swooping low,*
> *would strike me in the head*
> *and let*
> *Peirenean songs gush forth . . .*

But alas, no breeze, no bronzed cicadas,
wherewith to thank you for your songs
and for their dedication

> *in which I share, with Nathan,*
> *the largess of your spirit and*
> *the blessing of your song . . .*

> *But graces such as these*
> *are not the fashion now. Our times*

*are Ginsburg, and the yawp and howl
is out upon our large dissensions,
as though to heal by bawl and outrage—
King Herod with a beard mistook
for Jeremiah (who, perhaps, wore none).
The bows we draw are shafted at
Canaveral. We do not see
Diana in the moon; we drive
our golf-balls at the lunar new
horizon . . .*

    *(Yet, like poets, they were near
    the brinks of terror, and they saw
    the mythless earth in blue
    formality—the singular
    small body of our hopes and fears,
    blue-white and wind-swept
    swung aloft—particular
    and beautiful, a pale oasis in
    a drift of stars . . .)*

*Alternatives are grass
and red wheelbarrows . . .*

It seems sometimes

    *that art, like shale,
    breaks up the hardened strata of
    life's former flows, and we—
    like children on a supervised
    inspection tour at some
    arcane museum—retrieve
    the chips, admire the bones
    of former glories; we
    gather up the shards
    and arrowheads of antique griefs
    and pain, and so become
    collectors, troglodytes
    of arms and power, the ant (h)-*

ropologists and ants of time.
The gods from time to time vouchsafe
some lucky find—a hieroglyph,
a bison on the cave-wall—and
we know quite well the Logos'
signature is on the deep
and in the sleep
of unloved Psyche ere she goes
to fetch her hank of wool
from those shining rams (so golden)
of the sun . . .

                and we wonder once again
what Phoenix nests, what Calvarys,
we callously pass by.

In your verses I have seen

    a whiteness like the Parthenon;
and sometimes, too, I think I hear
the ripple of still waters, or
the shimmering pools of Siloam, where
occurred that healing of the eyes
that you and I both know of . . .

Privilege enough, with thanks,

    to share
the place where David's
lightnings flare
to feel these graces
bound in me
or from these Delphis
glimpse the sea.

                               Stanley Romaine Hopper
                               1975

A POEM FOR AMOS WILDER

I

Nowhere do leaves come down
Out of the giant trees
Without, perhaps, catching in
Their winding down some ending
Not to come again. So goodbyes
        Sadden on the air and sing
The wry mythologies of mankind
Being to the last but man.

Yet, think you how, free of
Dense foliage and summer honors
However green and golden—
In its simplicities an elm
Becomes a window, an oak a space
Through which again we see,
Immense and necessary,
New sceneries, new ways for love:

Light such as winter sends aslant
Out of the short sun's breath,
Mercies of meadows running on and far,
And all the margins of the world
Set free. O celebrate how man,
Taking his next season boldly,
Feels huge assurance, expects
The distant mountains to be true.

II

I thinking of you minding in love
The poet's trade: the words we spoke,
The fires we set, the birds flown out,
The spires trimmed up, the sound
Drums drumming north and south

And back and forth. Our doubt
You knew and always cared about.

You with your Greek and heavy books
Were never lost in scholar's tricks.
You heard, as we did, underground,
God gathering in the shabby nights
Our chips of faith, our hate of sham,
Accepting azure poems we wrote
To exorcise our suburb guilt.

I saw once in a salt stream
The blue fisherman, heron and tall,
Walking the waters precisely. He
Prowled for hours the cold sea,
Then lifted clumsily his stilts,
Managed the climbing air and rose—
Easily, silently, hopefully going.

       December 10, 1963
       Arnold Kenseth

WILDERIANA
Dates and Places

It is suggested that readers would be helped if the allusions to my work in the conversation and the Comment were placed in some sort of context. For younger readers especially this kind of chronology and map may suggest the experience of many of us the greater part of whose life was lived before WW II.

Family. Born 1895, Madison, Wisconsin. Father, a journalist with a Yale Ph.D., later in the consular service in China, returning to this country in 1914 as head of Yale-in-China. Mother: Isabella Niven, daughter of Presbyterian minister, Dobbs Ferry, N.Y. Family nurture: Bunyan, George Fox, etc. in family devotions, and the influences of our mother's accomplishments in French, Italian and music. Five children. One sister, Yale Drama School and novelist; another, English department at Wheaton College and Smith, and national poetry prize (Shelley Memorial Award, with Ben Belit); another,

Ph.D. in biology and teacher at Mt. Holyoke. Brother, Thornton Wilder. Married, Catherine Kerlin of Moorestown, N.J. 1935. After graduating from Smith in 1929, she had several years of international experience in Geneva, Switzerland, including teaching.

Education. Yale B.A. 1920, but my first two years at Oberlin. Yale B.D. 1924, but the first two years at Mansfield College, Oxford (including a summer at Toynbee Hall, London). Yale Ph.D. (1935) in New Testament (including one year at Harvard). One year as Belgian-American Fellow at the University of Brussels (1920–21). Highlights of these years of education would be a year of travel and tutoring which extended to India and the Near East (1924–25). Also the associations and summer "Weeks of Work" of the (then) Society for Religion in Higher Education. Here in retrospect one can recognize the beginnings and the shaping spirits of what became the American Academy of Religion and such inter-disciplinary areas as theology-and-literature.

War Service. With hundreds of others I interrupted my college years by serving in the American Ambulance Field Service in France in 1916. In 1917 I was for several months in the same service in Macedonia. Since America was now in the War, I left the Field Service and was inducted as a private in the U.S. Field Artillery, and served in a battery (and later in regimental headquarters) until the spring of 1919. I have written of my war experience, including notes from my diaries, together with remarks on the question of pacifism, in my paper, "At the Nethermost Piers of History: World War I, A View from the Ranks," published in George A. Panichas (ed) *Promise of Greatness: The War of 1914–1918*, New York: John Day, 1968, pp. 344–357.

New Testament Study and Teaching. After a pastorate in the Congregational Church, North Conway, N.H. (1925–

1928) with the help of a Kent Fellowship I chose graduate study in the field of the New Testament at Yale, with my interest directed to the relation of eschatology to ethics in the Gospels. At Mansfield College in Oxford in 1922 I had been drawn to this topic by contact with Albert Schweitzer. When he lectured at the College I served as his secretary briefly. I can see now that I was already interested in the imaginative and mythological aspects of apocalyptic, which I felt were misunderstood by the scholars. In later teaching at Andover Newton (1933–1943), Chicago (1943–1954) and Harvard (1954–1962) this interest widened to a more general interest in biblical theology and interpretation. With all my indebtedness to Rudolf Bultmann I took issue both with existentialist and liberal approaches. My presidential address to the Society of Biblical Literature in 1955 was entitled, "Scholars, Theologians and Ancient Rhetoric." In this period I had many contacts with European centers and shared in the World Council of Churches committees dealing with hermeneutics and with the Church and the Jewish People.

Poetry and Literary Interests. The mainline churches after WW I were still Victorian in their arts and tastes. My interest in the new writing of the time led to my being invited to talk to the clergy and church groups about these strange new voices. This led to my teaching in this field and to my first books on the new poetry and modern literature. Later Marvin Halverson headed up the section on religion and the arts for the National Council of Churches, and drew many of us into contacts with leading artists and writers. This activity continued in the Society for the Arts, Religion and Contemporary Culture which became less church-oriented and more concerned with values in the total culture.

My own stance in these later discussions—as represented also in my Tillich Lectures (in *The New Voice*) and in my verse—goes back to my biblical orientation, as I have noted in the interview. I recognize with the great modern emancipators and iconoclasts how many old tyrannies in society and in the soul need to be demasked. I recognize how much inhumanity can be accumulated in religious traditions which once were liberating. I recognize how parochial our Western mental and spiritual habits can be, and what varieties of human creativity and wisdom can be enjoyed in other cultures. Therefore I do not defend particular dogmas, and I recognize that many men and women live by a deeper faith than they can formulate. But my war experience and my life experience have seemed to teach me some priorities. One of these is that salvation has to be political; it is not enough for the soul to be enlightened. Another is that liberation and emancipation are not enough, as we envisage them. There is a deeper liberation called for which costs a great deal more.

www.ingramcontent.com/pod-product-compliance
Lightning Source LLC
LaVergne TN
LVHW051711080426
835511LV00017B/2853